Bucket List
for couples

This Book belongs to

Brandon Senn

and

Sarah Senn

Love,
uncle mel
&
Auntie Car

This is our most beautiful photo together

This is our funniest photo together

Buck List
50 EXAMPLES

♡ 1. HAVE A Tech-Free DATE DAY TOGETHER

2. *Plan Your Future* ♡

_____

_____

_____

_____

_____

_____

_____

_____

3. *Stargaze on a* Rooftop

4. Write each other a short **LOVE** Letter

5. GO ON A DOUBLE Date

6. Visit each others Hometowns

7. Cook Dinner Together

8. **HAVE A PICNIC**

♡ 9. Take a **Workout** Class Together

♡ 10. **TAKE A** Spontaneous **ROAD TRIP**

11. *Do a movie marathon* ♡
WHICH MOVIE?

_____

_____

_____

_____

_____

_____

12. *Get Naughty in every* ♡
Room in your House

50 EXAMPLES

13. Say 100 times I LOVE YOU

14. STAY UP all Night

15. Sing a Karaoke Duet

16. Come up with pet names for each other

17. TAKE A Trip SOMEWHERE NEW

18. Sleep Under the STAR

19. CREATE A Monogram AND LEAVE YOUR MARK

20. Start a new TRADITION together and write down!

_____

_____

_____

_____

_____

_____

_____

21. Dress up in a couples costume for Halloween

50 EXAMPLES

22. Do a Spaghetti **KISS** ♡

♡ 23. PLAY MINI Golf

24. Kiss on Top of a ♡
Ferris Wheel

♡ 25. *Watch the Sunset and Sunrise in one Day*

26. **GO BOWLING** ♡

50 EXAMPLES

27. Take a **Bubble Bath**

28. MAKE LOVE IN AN EXCITING LOCATION

29. *Create a Music Playlist of Your Relationship*

WRITE DOWN THE TOP 5

_____

_____

_____

_____

_____

30. *Go to the* Beach

31. Create a couple SCRAPBOOK

32. Dine out at a Fancy Restaurant

33. Take a Hot Air Balloon Ride

34. Cover the bed in rose petals

35. HAVE HANGOVER TOGETHER

♡ 36. Recreate Your
First Date

♡ 37. Cliff Jump WHILE Holding Hands

38. Make Thanksgiving ♡ Dinner

39. Go Shopping ♡

♡ 40. Dance in the **RAIN**

50 EXAMPLES

41. CUDDLE BY THE FIRE

42. Take a Tandem
Bike Ride

43. Join the mile
High Club

44. LEARN TO TANGO

45. KISS IN THE RAIN

♡ 46. Have Breakfast  in Bed

♡ 47. Complete a PUZZLE Together

48. Get a couple massage ♡

49. Go Wine Tasting ♡

♡ 50. Dance in the KITCHEN

50 EXAMPLES

Now its your turn

_____ ♡

_____

♡ _____

_____

_____ ♡

_____

♡ _____

_____

_____ ♡

_____

Lets Start
Our Bucket List
100 THINGS
WE WANT TO
DO TOGETHER

Page

01		
02		
03		
04		
05		
06		
07		
08		
09		
10		
11		
12		
13		
14		
15		

Page

16 ....
17 ....
18 ....
19 ....
20 ....
21 ....
22 ....
23 ....
24 ....
25 ....
26 ....
27 ....
28 ....
29 ....
30 ....
31 ....
32 ....
33 ....
34 ....
35 ....
36 ....
37 ....
38 ....
39 ....
40 ....

41 ....

42 ....

43 ....

44 ....

45 ....

46 ....

47 ....

48 ....

49 ....

50 ....

51 ....

52 ....

53 ....

54 ....

55 ....

56 ....

57 ....

58 ....

59 ....

60 ....

61 ....

62 ....

63 ....

64 ....

65 ....

Page

66 ....
67 ....
68 ....
69 ....
70 ....
71 ....
72 ....
73 ....
74 ....
75 ....
76 ....
77 ....
78 ....
79 ....
80 ....
81 ....
82 ....
83 ....
84 ....
85 ....
86 ....
87 ....
88 ....
89 ....
90 ....

91 ....

92 ....

93 ....

94 ....

95 ....

96 ....

97 ....

98 ....

99 ....

100 ....

Photo

I cant wait to see where else our love will lead us.

This is our plan

01

We did it

Date completed

Location

Storytime

This is our plan

02

 We did it

Date completed .... Location ....

Storytime ....

This is our plan

03

We did it

Date completed .... Location ....

Storytime ....

This is our plan

04

....

....

....

 ## We did it

Date completed .... Location ....

Storytime ....

....

....

....

....

....

....

....

....

This is our plan

05

We did it

Date completed .... Location ....

Storytime ....

This is our plan

06

....

....

....

 **We did it**

Date completed .... Location ....

Storytime ....

....

....

....

....

....

....

....

This is our plan

We did it

Date completed

Location

Storytime

This is our plan

08

We did it

Date completed

Location

Storytime

This is our plan

09

We did it

Date completed

Location

Storytime

This is our plan

10

We did it

Date completed .... Location ....

Storytime ....

This is our plan

11

We did it

Date completed

Location

Storytime

This is our plan

12

 ## We did it

Date completed .... Location ....

Storytime ....

This is our plan

13

We did it

Date completed

Location

Storytime

This is our plan

14

....

....

....

We did it

Date completed .... Location ....

Storytime ....

....

....

....

....

....

....

....

This is our plan

15

We did it

Date completed

Location

Storytime

This is our plan

16

We did it

Date completed .... Location ....

Storytime ....

This is our plan

17

We did it

Date completed

Location

Storytime

This is our plan

18

 We did it

Date completed .... Location ....

Storytime ....

This is our plan

19

We did it

Date completed .... Location ....

Storytime ....

....
....
....
....
....
....

This is our plan

20

....
....
....

 **We did it**

Date completed .... Location ....

Storytime ....
....
....
....
....
....
....
....

This is our plan

21

We did it

Date completed .... Location ....

Storytime ....

....

....

....

....

....

....

....

This is our plan

22

We did it

Date completed .... Location ....

Storytime ....

....

....

....

....

....

....

....

This is our plan

23

We did it

Date completed

Location

Storytime

This is our plan

24

We did it

Date completed .... Location  ....

Storytime ....
....
....
....
....
....
....
....
....

This is our plan

25

We did it

Date completed

Location

Storytime

This is our plan

26

We did it

Date completed .... Location ....

Storytime ....

This is our plan

27

We did it

Date completed .... Location ....

Storytime ....

This is our plan

28

We did it

Date completed .... Location ....

Storytime ....

This is our plan

29

We did it

Date completed

Location

Storytime

This is our plan

30

We did it

Date completed .... Location ....

Storytime ....

This is our plan

We did it

Date completed .... Location ....

Storytime ....

....

....

....

....

....

....

This is our plan

32

We did it

Date completed .... Location ....

Storytime ....

This is our plan

33

We did it

Date completed

Location

Storytime

This is our plan

34

....

....

....

We did it

Date completed .... Location ....

Storytime ....

....

....

....

....

....

....

....

....

This is our plan

35

We did it

Date completed

Location

Storytime

This is our plan

36

 We did it

Date completed .... Location ....

Storytime ....

This is our plan

37

 ## We did it

Date completed .... Location ....

Storytime ....

This is our plan

38

We did it

Date completed .... Location ....

Storytime ....

This is our plan

39

We did it

Date completed

Location

Storytime

This is our plan

40

 **We did it**

Date completed .... Location ....

Storytime ....

This is our plan

41

We did it

Date completed

Location

Storytime

This is our plan

42

We did it

Date completed

Location

Storytime

This is our plan

43

We did it

Date completed .... Location ....

Storytime ....

This is our plan

44

 We did it

Date completed .... Location ....

Storytime ....
....
....
....
....
....
....
....

This is our plan

45

We did it

Date completed .... Location ....

Storytime ....

This is our plan

46

 We did it

Date completed

Location

Storytime

This is our plan

47

We did it

Date completed .... Location ....

Storytime ....

This is our plan

48

We did it

Date completed .... Location ....

Storytime ....

This is our plan

49

We did it

Date completed .... Location ....

Storytime ....

This is our plan

We did it

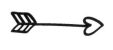

Date completed

Location

Storytime

This is our plan

51

We did it

Date completed .... Location ....

Storytime ....

This is our plan

 **We did it**

Date completed .... Location ....

Storytime ....

....

....

....

....

....

....

....

This is our plan

53

We did it

Date completed .... Location ....

Storytime ....

This is our plan

54

 ## We did it

Date completed .... Location ....

Storytime ....

This is our plan

55

We did it

Date completed .... Location ....

Storytime ....

This is our plan

56

We did it

Date completed .... *Location* ....

Storytime ....

....

....

....

....

....

....

....

This is our plan

57

We did it

Date completed

Location

Storytime

This is our plan

58

We did it

Date completed .... Location ....

Storytime ....

This is our plan

59

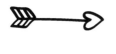 We did it

Date completed

Location

Storytime

This is our plan

60

We did it

Date completed .... Location ....

Storytime ....

This is our plan

61

We did it

Date completed .... Location ....

Storytime ....
....
....
....
....
....
....
....
....

This is our plan

62

 We did it

Date completed .... Location ....

Storytime ....

....

....

....

....

....

....

....

This is our plan

63

We did it

Date completed .... Location ....

Storytime ....

This is our plan

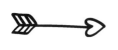 **We did it**

Date completed .... Location ....

Storytime ....

....

....

....

....

....

....

....

This is our plan

65

We did it

Date completed .... Location ....

Storytime ....

66

This is our plan

We did it

Date completed .... Location ....

Storytime ....

....

....

....

....

....

....

....

....

....

....

This is our plan

67

We did it

Date completed .... Location ....

Storytime ....

This is our plan

68

We did it

Date completed .... Location ....

Storytime ....

....

....

....

....

....

....

This is our plan

69

We did it

Date completed .... Location ....

Storytime ....

This is our plan

70

We did it

Date completed .... Location ....

Storytime ....
....
....
....
....
....
....
....
....

This is our plan

71

We did it

Date completed .... Location ....

Storytime ....

72

This is our plan

....

....

....

 ## We did it

Date completed .... Location ....

Storytime ....

....

....

....

....

....

....

This is our plan

73

We did it

Date completed .... Location

Storytime ....

This is our plan

74

We did it

Date completed .... Location ....

Storytime ....

This is our plan

75

We did it

Date completed .... Location ....

Storytime ....

This is our plan

76

We did it

Date completed _____ Location _____

Storytime _____

This is our plan

77

We did it

Date completed .... Location ....

Storytime ....

78

This is our plan

 ## We did it

Date completed

Location

Storytime

This is our plan

79

We did it

Date completed .... Location ....

Storytime ....

This is our plan

80

We did it

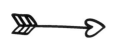 

Date completed

Location

Storytime

This is our plan

We did it

Date completed .... Location ....

Storytime ....

....

....

....

....

....

....

....

82

This is our plan

....

....

....

 ## We did it

Date completed .... Location ....

Storytime ....

....

....

....

....

....

....

....

This is our plan

83

We did it

Date completed .... Location ....

Storytime ....

This is our plan

84

 ## We did it

Date completed .... Location ....

Storytime ....

This is our plan

85

We did it

Date completed .... Location ....

Storytime ....

....

....

....

....

....

....

....

....

This is our plan

....

....

....

 ## We did it

Date completed .... Location ....

Storytime ....

....

....

....

....

....

....

This is our plan

87

 We did it

Date completed

Location

Storytime

This is our plan

88

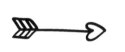 ## We did it

Date completed

Location

Storytime

This is our plan

89

We did it

Date completed .... Location ....

Storytime ....

....

....

....

....

....

....

....

This is our plan

....

....

....

 # We did it

Date completed .... *Location* ....

Storytime ....

....

....

....

....

....

....

This is our plan

91

We did it

Date completed .... Location

Storytime ....

This is our plan

 ## We did it

Date completed .... Location ....

Storytime ....

....
....
....
....
....
....

This is our plan

93

We did it

Date completed .... Location ....

Storytime ....

This is our plan

 ## We did it

Date completed .... **Location** ....

Storytime ....

This is our plan

95

We did it

Date completed .... Location ....

Storytime ....

96

This is our plan

 ## We did it

Date completed

Location

Storytime

This is our plan

97

We did it

Date completed .... Location ....

Storytime ....

This is our plan

98

We did it

 Date completed .... Location ....

Storytime ....

This is our plan

99

We did it

Date completed .... Location ....

Storytime ....

This is our plan

100

 ## We did it

Date completed

Location

Storytime

IMPRESSUM

Bei Fragen & Anregungen:
feedback@mertens-publication.de

1. Auflage

© 2018 Mertens Verlagsgruppe

Mertens Ventures Ltd.
Tinou 18, C02
7040 Oroklini
Zypern

E-Mail: kontakt@mertens-publication.de

Cover Design: Freepik at www.freepik.com
Icon made by Freepik from www.flaticon.com
Vector by Free at www.freepik.com

Made in the USA
San Bernardino, CA
13 November 2019